OVERCOMING TRAUMA
THROUGH CHRIST

How I overcame rape, escaped murder, attempted rape, and sexual abuse.

Discover the Power of Faith and Healing to Overcome Trauma and Find Wholeness in Christ.

Vinnette Smart-Bruney

Overcoming Trauma Through Christ: How I overcame rape, escaped murder, attempted rape, and sexual abuse.

Copyright © 2023 Vinnette Bruney

All rights reserved. No part of this book may be reproduced or transmitted in any form or by any means without the written permission of the author.

Scriptures marked KJV are taken from the KING JAMES VERSION (KJV): KING JAMES VERSION, public domain.

Scripture taken from the New King James Version®. Copyright © 1982 by Thomas Nelson. Used by permission. All rights reserved.

Scripture quotations marked (NIV) are taken from the Holy Bible, New International Version®, NIV®. Copyright © 1973, 1978, 1984, 2011 by Biblica, Inc.™ Used by permission of Zondervan.

All rights reserved worldwide. www.zondervan.com. The "NIV" and "New International Version" are trademarks registered in the United States Patent and Trademark Office by Biblica, Inc.™.

Scriptures marked AMP are taken from the AMPLIFIED BIBLE (AMP): Scripture taken from the AMPLIFIED® BIBLE, Copyright © 1954, 1958, 1962, 1964, 1965, 1987 by the Lockman Foundation Used by Permission. (www.Lockman.org)

Published by:
Eleviv Publishing Group
Centerville, OH 45458
info@elevivpublishing.com
www.elevivpublishing.com

ISBN: (PB) 978-1-952744-77-8
        (E-book) 978-1-952744-78-5
        Journal: 978-1-952744-79-2

Printed in the United States of America

Dedication

Yahweh, I truly love You! I am so grateful for everything you have done for me. Throughout my trauma and pain, You are always there. Thanks for never turning Your back on me.

In 2020, You told me through the Prophecy of Prophet Shamar to write this book and make my petition known because it will bring healing to many who have experienced or going through similar situations. I write this book in obedience to your words. Thank You, Lord! I give You all the Praise, Honor, Glory, and adoration.

Acknowledgement

Ephesians 3:20 states, God can do exceedingly abundantly above all that we ask or think according to the power that worketh in us.

First, I want to give God thanks for blessing Romaine and Annie with my beautiful, joyful grandson Cole.
To my sons Romaine and Kadeem, I love you both very much. I truly admire your ability to stay strong despite all we have been through as a family.

Romaine, when I finally revealed my traumatic experience to you, you did not dig for details or judge me but encouraged me to tell my story. Thanks for being supportive and understanding. I am sure Kadeem will be as supportive when he's better able to understand.

Thanks to you, my sweet mom Imogene, for your love and support throughout the years. Many thanks to aunt Laurel for filling the position as my mother when mom migrated to the USA in search of a better life, and to aunt Lynn (R.I.P), for your counseling, for your kindness, and for allowing me a safe space in your home.

To my brother Vittel for stepping up when our father passed away. I am genuinely grateful to you for paving the pathway to the USA for a better life for me, mom, and all our siblings. To my sister Dr. Paulette M., I appreciate you for encouraging me to write this book to tell my story and for all your support. To all my siblings, family and friends, thanks for all your care throughout the years. May God bless you all continuously.

Table of Contents

Prologue

Foreword

Introduction

Chapter 1:
The Nature of Trauma
My Story of Pain, Trauma, and Grief... *16*

Chapter 2:
The Nature of Trauma II
Murder, and how I escaped murder, attempted rape, and sexual abuse... *34*

Chapter 3:
Faith and Healing
The role of faith in the healing process... *51*

Chapter 4:
Overcoming Obstacles
Recognizing and confronting obstacles to healing... *60*

Chapter 5:
Forgiveness and Compassion
Cultivating Healing and Wholeness... *67*

Chapter 6:
Loving God through the Pain
... 73

Chapter 7:
Sharing Your Story
The Message in your Mess... *77*

Chapter 8:
Moving Forward
Finding hope and joy in the future... *81*

Conclusion
Acknowledgements
About the Author

He heals the brokenhearted and binds up their wounds.
Psalm 147:3

Foreword

I am honored to write the foreword for this powerful and inspiring book on overcoming trauma through Christ. Trauma is a deeply personal and painful experience that can leave us feeling lost, broken, and alone. But through the pages of this book, we are reminded that we are never truly alone and that there is always hope for healing and restoration.

The stories contained within these pages are raw, honest, and deeply moving. They are a testament to the power of faith and the strength of the human spirit. From the depths of despair to the heights of hope, these stories show us that no matter how dark our experiences may be, there is always a path forward.

The author of this book is a brave and courageous individual who has faced trauma head-on and, through her faith in Christ, has found the strength to overcome. Her stories are a source of inspiration and encouragement for anyone who has faced trauma.

As a Christian Counselor and Missionary who has worked with many individuals who have faced trauma, I know firsthand the power of faith in the healing process.

When we trust in a power greater than ourselves, we tap into a source of strength and hope that can help us overcome even the most painful experiences.

This book is not just a collection of stories but a guide for those struggling to find their way through the aftermath of trauma. It reminds us that healing is possible, that we are not alone, and that there is always hope. Through the pages of this book, we are offered a roadmap for healing, a way forward toward a brighter future.

I am honored to write the foreword for this book and to have the opportunity to share this powerful story with the world. I know that they will offer hope and encouragement to anyone struggling with the aftermath of trauma. May this book be a source of comfort and strength for all who read it.

Vivian Elebiyo-Okojie

Prologue

Trauma has a way of taking hold of us, digging deep into our souls, and leaving us feeling broken and alone. It can happen in an instant, leaving a lasting impact on our lives. For some, the aftermath of trauma can be crippling, leaving them feeling like there is no way out. But there is hope. Through the love of Christ, we can find a path to healing and wholeness.

I found my healing through Christ as a woman of faith who has overcome the worst of situations and become stronger and more resilient in my walk with Christ. God never promised us a life without darkness; He promised us His presence and light when we experience darkness.

When you go through deep waters, I will be with you. When you go through rivers of difficulty, you will not drown. When you walk through the fire of oppression, you will not be burned up; the flames will not consume you. Isaiah 43:2 (NLT)

His promise is to always be with us, even through the worst situations. There is healing through Christ if we allow Him to help us heal. The journey to healing is a challenging one. It requires us to confront our pain and our deepest fears. It demands that we trust in a power greater than ourselves, a power that can provide us with the strength to face our demons and overcome them. It takes courage to walk this path, to be vulnerable and honest about the wounds inflicted upon us. But it is through this courage that we can begin to rebuild ourselves piece by piece until we stand firm once again.

    This book is a guide for those who are struggling to overcome the trauma they have experienced. It is a collection of my stories, struggles, triumphs, hope, and faith. You will find the tools you need to begin the healing process through these pages. You will learn to embrace your faith and trust in Christ to give you the strength to face your pain. You will discover how to cultivate a positive mindset and surround yourself with supportive people who can help you. You will find inspiration and encouragement from my story as I have walked this path before you and have emerged stronger and more resilient.

    This book is not just a collection of my stories of trauma, rape, and abuse but a testament to the power of Christ and his ability to heal even the deepest wounds. It is a reminder that you are not alone in your struggles and that there is hope for a brighter tomorrow. There is a way forward no matter what trauma you have faced or how broken you may feel. Through Christ, you can find the strength to overcome, heal, and move forward into a brighter, more hopeful future.

Introduction

Trauma is a universal human experience. It can take many forms and affect us in countless ways. It can leave us feeling broken, lost, and alone. But it is possible to find healing and hope, even in the aftermath of the most painful experiences. The key to this healing is faith in Christ.

This book shares my stories, insights, and practical tools for those who are seeking to overcome trauma through the power of Christ. It is an invitation to embrace the hope and healing that is available to us all, no matter what we have experienced.

As someone who has experienced trauma in many different forms, faced abuse, and violence, and battled with defeating attitudes and thoughts. But despite all of the darkness- I found the healing light of God and developed a deep faith in Christ and a belief in the power of healing through Him.

Through the pages of this book, you will hear my stories of struggle and triumph. You will be inspired by my courage and resilience in the face of pain and adversity. You will learn from my experiences, gaining insight and understanding into the complex nature of trauma and the healing process.

This book isn't just a book to share my journey and the pain of it, but a roadmap for those who are seeking a path to healing and wholeness. It offers practical tools, resources, and biblical references for overcoming obstacles and finding hope in the midst of suffering. It is a reminder that we are not alone in our struggles, and that there is always a way forward.

I hope that this book will be a source of inspiration and encouragement for all who read it. Whether you are in the midst of a personal struggle or seeking to support a loved one, I believe that you will find something of value within these pages. May the Holy Spirit guide you through your healing process, as He did mine. May you be strengthened and encouraged on your journey towards healing and restoration in Jesus' name.

Chapter 1

The Nature of Trauma

My Story of Pain, Trauma, and Grief

When you go through deep waters, I will be with you. When you go through rivers of difficulty, you will not drown. When you walk through the fire of oppression, you will not be burned up; the flames will not consume you. Isaiah 43:2 (NLT)

At the age of 16, I experienced one of the most horrible crimes a woman could ever experience, which is rape. I was raped at gunpoint by two gangsters while travelling to my bus stop to take a bus home. The setting took place in Jamaica. It was in the heat of the election in Jamaica with two major political parties, PNP and JLP, competing (battling) against each other for what seemed like a rally and support of the people but truly for hidden agendas.

I visited my brother, sister, and family; it was time to go home, and due to the violent nature of the elections, my brother had to decide whether to follow me to the bus stop within walking distance, about two miles each way from home, where I could take a bus home or to put me on the bus going downtown Kingston, to take a second bus home. The thought of staying overnight didn't even cross my mind, nor did it occur to my siblings because the house was crowded. I was also afraid of getting in trouble with my aunt, with whom I was staying with.

Cell phones were not part of technological advancement at the time, and if they were, they would not be affordable according to our financial status at the time. There was no phone to call home to tell my aunt I would not be home for the night, and it would have seemed disrespectful if I didn't notify her. It would seem as if it was my original plan. Oh yeah! There were the corded home phones; the ones you could hear ringing from far away would wake the entire house when it rang, but not many people could afford them. Car was not an option because it was unaffordable, and no one owned a driver's license in the house.

My brother accompanied me to the closest bus stop to take the bus to downtown Kingston to get on another bus to get home (home was in Portmore, a suburban area) outside Kingston. Getting from one bus stop to another was a distance away. Downtown Kingston was very scanty with people in comparison to daytime. It was late at night, and I was walking fast to get to the next bus stop due to fear of attackers.

Sometimes your fear can become your worst nightmare, because while walking fast to escape attackers, the enemy had a plan. I walked right into two gangsters coming directly from where I was heading. I was so close to the bus stop I was walking to; Gosh! I could see the buses waiting there. The next thing I heard was to turn around, keep walking, don't make any noise; we have guns, Do not scream or create excitement. This is the best I can remember, and those words have stuck in my head for years.

I walked with them to a remote and rundown area which I now believe to be the Tivoli Garden area. They took me to a dilapidated and ran-down abandoned house, where they proceeded to rape me; each taking turns while the other looked out for other gangsters who might creep up on them or possibly the cops or the army.

It is very prevalent for cops to patrol the streets and raid gang-infested areas, especially during election times. The army usually dispenses its armed forces to assist, when things become too overwhelming for the cops to handle.

Gangsters seem to respect and fear the armed forces more than the cops. Gangsters kill cops just as much as they do civilians or each other because they have not much regard for them. There are some good cops in the area, but there are also some very corrupt ones who usually get themselves involved in various illicit activities; but they will take the gangsters down before the gangsters get to them first.

The two rapers took advantage of me for approximately an hour or two, but it seemed like forever, in this dark run-down house lying on my back on the floor, but mostly backwards on my knees pleasuring themselves, but were very antsy, because they knew death could knock at their door in seconds; even though it was knocking at mine , but I stood and the promises that *"God has not given me a Spirit of Fear, but a Spirit of Power, a Spirit of Love, and a Spirit of Sound Mind." (Isaiah 54:17 KJV)*.

While one of them was taking advantage of me, I could hear the other conversing with another guy outside the house about other gangsters' activities (the house were close to each other; they were tenement yards). I could hear what seemed to be the sounds of gunshots from a distance, but being raped by two gangsters was far more heartwrenching. There were much more to worry about having two gangsters with guns raping me, not knowing if they would kill me when done, or if they were carrying diseases and could possibly give them to me. Thank God HIV/Aids was not discovered at the time, or it wasn't secretly in existence.

My most prominent thought and fear was survival. I knew they had guns, so my strategy for survival was to cooperate with them and allow them to take advantage of me without screaming, crying, fighting, and cursing. They would probably kill me if I brought attention to them or the situation. Using curse words at them didn't cross my path because I am not one to use curse words, neither was I much of a fighter, and it honestly wouldn't do much for me.

I was up against two rapists with guns. Staying alive was the key because no one would know where to find me or where to recover my body. Cursing was not a part of my upbringing, so I didn't practice it. Mom especially raised her children with the fear of God, and the only people I ever fought with were my siblings growing up and a girl in elementary school in Kingston.

I avoided fights at all costs because I didn't like people hitting me. Getting beat by my parents, principal, and teachers was more than enough.

My attackers did not ask many questions; if they asked any, I cannot remember. They weren't interested in talking much but in pleasuring themselves and moving on to their next prey or activity.

They decided to walk me to the bus stop when they finished taking advantage of me. They wanted to ensure I did not report them to the authority or tell anyone. They threatened me that if I told the authorities or told anyone, they would do what they had to do. I promised them I would not tell anyone as they walked me to the bus stop in the late hours of the night to catch probably the last bus home.

I was frightened and traumatic as I could not believe what had just happened to me. God saved my life. I was in a state of disbelief as I walked in the still quietness of the night with two gangsters who had just finished raping me, and then chose to walk side by side with me to my bus stop like we were buddies. I didn't have time to look down at my white pants to see the dirt and stains on them as I pulled it up and zipped them up to cover my lower body because time was of the essence.

Gangsters are always on the go; they cannot tarry too long in one place because the authorities and other gangsters seek to kill them. Even though they put up this toughness upfront, beneath all that upfront toughness and evil is fear; the fear of running into the wrong people at the wrong time. I realized their strength was of the devil;

their strength is in the guns they were carrying. The devil strengthens them to use them to do evil; to carry out these evil missions, which can and will result in harsh punishments or death for them. It must be so miserable and tormenting for any human to live their lives that way.

I cannot remember how long it took to get a bus, but I remember it was a long, painful and miserable ride home. As I sat on the bus into the light, I looked down at my white pants and quickly realized how disgusting and dirty they looked. It's a good thing the bus wasn't crowded. I was so ashamed. The kind of shame you feel when you do something wrong, something out of character. You see, the enemy quickly tried to manipulate my mind into believing I did something wrong, to believe it was my fault. Two gangsters brutally raped me, and the devil wanted me to believe it was my fault. Look at you now! How dirty and disgusting you look! The devil is a liar, *"because greater is He that is in me than he that is in the world." (1 John 4:4 KJV)*

It was so traumatizing to think about what to say to my aunt when I got home. I felt like I was sleeping, and this was just a dream. Like what in the world just happened to me! Is this real? I wished I had woken up, and it was only a dream. I was at a loss all the way home. Which was fortunate for me; I didn't want anyone to see my messed-up white pants. I don't know how I was aware of getting off at the right bus stop, because I was lost in my thoughts as it seemed like my world caved in on me.

I walked home in the still of the night as I got off the bus. It must have been approximately 12:45 am, but it seemed later. The only noise I heard was that of bugs, insects and birds because there were no humans on the road. The walk home was approximately three minutes, and I couldn't even remember walking home. I knew I did, but I was in a discombobulated state of mind.

My aunt opened the door after I knocked; I entered the living room, and she locked the front door. I was in much of a safety zone. She looked at me with a sense of bewilderment and shock. She saw how messy my pants were. I started crying while telling her two guys held me at gunpoint and raped me in a secluded building in downtown Kingston. She was really shocked and confused as to how to handle the situation. I remember my cousin came out of bed as she was curious about what was going on because she had woken up from the loudness of the conversation. They proceeded to get the next-door neighbor, who was a cop, but nothing was done to report the incident to the authorities that night, the following day, or ever.

After talking to him about my traumatic story, the next day, I learned from my aunt that he (the cop) did not believe my story was true. He, a cop, did not further try to investigate the incident or even encourage me to go to the authorities because, in his state of mind, he did not believe the incident was true. Just because he didn't believe it doesn't mean it didn't happen.

I did not understand then because I was sixteen and did not know about or even spoken to any rape victims. I knew rape was a common assault amongst the female counterpart, but they never openly discussed it. After being a victim myself, I realized later that women don't speak about this traumatic experience, not only because of the trauma it brought to their lives, but because no one believes, or would believe their stories. Therefore, we are forced to wrap up this demon in a blanket like a baby, and carry it inside our bellies and hearts for the rest of our lives, and even take it to our graves, because talking about it only shames us and makes a liar out of us.

I am led to believe it's my fault why it happened, while I shut down from being this spunky happy person to being someone who was lost, quiet and ashamed, wishing I could turn the clock back to where it never happened. This Cop next door, who tried to shut down my story, was married with children at the time but was very perverted. He would always come to the fence between our house and his when he saw me sitting on the carport, to make sexual advances. He must have seen this as an act of revenge because I never allowed him to take advantage of me. I would shut him down with a no or ignore him each time. The man who frequently put on a display with his wife on their carport, or someplace on the lawn around the house, lying down on blankets, showing what seemed to be affection with each other, but behind the scene, very perverted.

The attitude of this cop next door showed how people could cover up their own demons, hide their skeletons in their closets, and deflect their actions on others, especially victims. Only God knows how many young girls had fallen prey to him or he took advantage of the way he tried to take advantage of me. My rape situation probably made him felt guilty about what he must have done to other females, so he quickly shut my situation down to quiet the demon inside of him, so he can feel better about his own actions. The traumatic situation occurred on a Saturday, so a few days later, my aunt took me to the doctor to perform an examination. After the examination, my aunt was involved in a private conversation with the doctor, and nothing was mentioned to me about the doctor's conclusion.

I remember my aunt took me to a friend's house, a neighboring house on a different street, to phone my mum here in the U.S. to tell her about my traumatic situation. It was quite humiliating for me, because everyone in the house could hear the conversation. I also remember sobbing as I tried to get the words out of my mouth. Needless to say, it was never really mentioned again. It was like the rape situation never took place. No one took the time to ask me how I was doing, how I was feeling or how I was coping. It just got swept under the rug. It was a mixed emotion for me at the time, because in one way, I wanted to know that they cared, but on the other hand, I just wanted to be left alone and block it out of my memory. It became easier for me to put up a mental block since no one brought it up or reminded me of it, but that was temporary.

While walking me to the bus stop, the guys told me to meet them the following Monday after school, at a location close to the bus stop. I was heading to the bus stop when I ran into them. I agreed to meet them because I was afraid to say no. Two of my brothers, who lived in Kingston at the time of occurrence, heard about the incident and decided to follow me to the designated location to meet up with them. My brothers were so angry and wanted to meet them face to face. I was not sure if my brothers had guns at the time, but I knew that the guys had guns because they were gangsters, and they raped me at gunpoint.

I was terrified not only for my safety but also for my brother's safety. They walked behind me, not too close, pretending they did not know me. All they wanted to do was to beat those guys down and teach them a harsh lesson. I knew my brothers could fight and run fast, and were also fast kickers, who could kick the guns from their hands, but that was taking a big risk. A bullet is much faster, unless of course you're a kung fu expert; but it's still risky regardless.

The gangster did not show up, either because they were afraid of me setting them up with the cops or they were somewhere else committing crimes, waiting for their next victim or plotting to. It was a bittersweet situation for me because I wanted to see my brothers deal with them severely, but on the other hand, I was happy they didn't have to get themselves in trouble, or be hurt during the process. My brothers were very much disappointed, because they were physically and mentally ready to face these demons, but it was not meant to be; God knows best.

I came face to face with one of the guys twice after my attacks. Once while going to the market with one of my older sisters. We were headed in opposite directions of the market, when he passed by me; and as I glanced back at him, he glanced back at me. My heart raced so fast, as I whispered to my sister, that one of the rapers just past by us. I tried to mask myself into the crowd while trying not to look back at him to bring attention to myself, or to remind him of who I was. My mind reflected on my brothers, thinking if they were with me at the moment, he would have surely gotten what he deserved.

My other encounter with one of the guys occurred one evening while walking downtown Kingston, again, to catch my bus to go home. This time I was coming from school. There were many people walking to and fro, and many cars driving back and forth. I believed I was walking with my friend, one of my schoolmates, when he approached me, walking in the opposite direction. He wanted to find out if I was the girl who put his friend in jail. I told him I had no idea what he was talking about, and acted like I was clueless. He was clueless as well, because he had no idea who I was. He did not remember me, like

I remembered him. My face seemed familiar to him for a different reason. I was the girl he raped, not the one that put his friend in jail; even though I wished I had put them both in jail. I'm not sure if he was talking about his partner in crime who raped me along with him, or someone else, but I do know it was my second time having an encounter with one without the other after my traumatic experience.

It doesn't surprise me his friend was in jail. Sooner or later, their actions would catch up with them. I can't imagine being the only female they have committed this vicious act of violence with; God's eyes are always watching, and he would make sure they get what they truly deserved. I have surrendered them to God. God is a master planner; He said, *"vengeance is mine, I will repay" (Romans 12:19)*. I had no doubt God has already judged them, and allowed His will to be done in their lives.

Being raped is one of the worst things a woman could endure. It puts a damper on your self-esteem and your mental, emotional, and physical state. It causes you to shut down, lose trust, and break your focus. I was no longer hanging out with the same friends, speaking much, and socializing as I used to. I became this sad person. I felt so alone. I needed someone to hug or tell me it was okay! I got you! Everything is going to be okay. I felt like it was me against the world. I felt lost, grossed, and robbed of my dignity. I wished when I went to sleep and woke up the next morning that it was only a dream; my imagination was only running wild. The hug, consolation, and love I was looking for, and longing for were nowhere to be found, because the close-knit family I grew up with got separated for a while until we migrated to the U.S.

If women could tell their stories, you'll find there would be no end to it because many have been abused in so many different ways; I'm sure likewise men could tell stories as well, but since this is about my experience, I'll focus on what women like myself go through. The pain of shame and the lack of support leads to years of loneliness, trauma bound, and addictions in a lot of women. I have heard stories of young girls and women, who took their own lives because of the pain and trauma they have experienced. Many women have been molested and raped numerous times; oftentimes by the same culprit for years, or by different culprits. the reoccurrence of rape is higher with women who have been raped before. At 16, I was completely lost from the pain of trauma, and I grieved my pain for years until I turned to God for help, and He healed me. I would definitely recommend anyone going through this traumatic situation to seek the help of God, because He can truly help you if you trust Him and believe. In addition, seeking the help of professional therapists is a definite recommendation.

Understanding trauma and its effects
Trauma is an experience that shatters our sense of safety, security, and well-being. It can be caused by various events, including physical or sexual abuse, domestic violence, natural disasters, accidents, illness, and more. Trauma can have profound and long-lasting effects on our mental, emotional, and physical health, as well as on our relationships, work, and other areas of our lives.

One of trauma's most challenging aspects is how it can make us feel isolated and alone. One of the first things that happened to me was the feeling of guilt, isolation, and loneliness. I felt it was my fault; then I felt my voice wasn't loud enough. I wasn't seen by those who loved me the most. Oftentimes, we may feel like no one else can understand what we are going through, or that we are somehow flawed or damaged. These feelings can be overwhelming and make it difficult to reach out for help and support.

But the truth is, that trauma is a common experience that affects many people. It is estimated that up to 70% of adults in the United States have experienced some form of trauma in their lifetime. This means that you are not alone in your struggle and that many others can relate to what you are going through.

The importance of acknowledging trauma
Recognizing the impact of trauma is an essential first step in the healing process. This means acknowledging trauma's effects on our mental, emotional, and physical well-being. Trauma can cause many symptoms, including anxiety, depression, hypervigilance, flashbacks, nightmares, and physical health problems. These symptoms can make it difficult to function daily, leading to feelings of shame,

guilt, and worthlessness.

Acknowledging the need for healing is also a crucial step in overcoming trauma. This means recognizing that healing is possible and that we are worthy of receiving help and support. It can be challenging to reach out for help, especially if we feel ashamed or embarrassed about what we have experienced. But seeking support is a sign of strength, not weakness, and can be a powerful step towards healing and recovery. Healing from trauma is a journey, and there is no one-size-fits-all approach.

Each person's experience of trauma is unique, and each person's path to healing will be different.

Finding the best tools and resources for you may take time, patience, and persistence. But with the support of loved ones may take time, patience, persistence, healthcare professionals, and deep faith in Christ, it is possible to find hope, healing, and wholeness after trauma.

Recognizing the need for healing.

You can read this first chapter and feel sorry for that 16-year-old girl walking to a bus stop whose life changed one night. There are several women and girls like me across the globe, some far younger and others far older. We all must heal from the pain of trauma if we must grow. God, in His word, says He desires, above all else, that we will be in good health and that our soul prospers. He desires for you and me to heal from life's scars. He wants us to no longer bleed over the wound we sustained during our journey through life. Trauma from the past can impede our growth, it might show up in our relationships, marriages, the way we raise our children, or deal with life and respond to issues. You must recognize the need for healing. It took me years to heal, but I did eventually.

In the following chapters, I will explore the role of faith in the healing process, offer tools and strategies for overcoming obstacles, and share stories of hope and triumph. I hope this book will be a source of inspiration and encouragement for all who have experienced trauma and offer a roadmap for the journey towards healing and restoration.

Chapter 2

The Nature of Trauma II

Murder, and How I escaped murder and attempted rape and sexual abuse

Be strong and courageous. Do not fear or be in dread of them, for it is the Lord your God who goes with you. He will not leave you or forsake you."(Deuteronomy 31:6-8)

My father got murdered one night, coming home from work when I was (12) twelve, and two (2) years later, my mother migrated to the United States to join my brother and his family, the brother who sponsored her to the United States. These two significant events, the former disastrous and the latter joyful and sad, caused our family to separate.

I say joyful because my mother's migrating to the U.S meant better lives for my siblings and me, but sadness because that nurturing mom was no longer around to run to, to ease my pain, my sadness, my boo-boo, and there was no surety of the period it would take to see her again.

It was indeed a bittersweet moment. I missed my mom the same day she left to board the plane to the US, and I miss my dad every day. My parents did not have much to give us regarding material things, but whatever they gave us, with the love on top, was more than enough. Money and material things are good while they last, but love, attention, and quality time are more effective and long-lasting. They were great parents; my dad was a fun-loving dad, who loved his children so much, and my mom continued to shower us with love.

The sudden death of my father while living in Jamaica was a great loss for our family and brought about trauma. He was the sole breadwinner for our big family of 17 (including Dad and Mom). My parents had eight boys and seven girls, including a set of twins, a boy, and a girl, but the boy passed away when he was approximately 18 months old. They took and raised as their child, a son from my father's sister, who could no longer care for him because he was very ill.

My father was a cop by profession and a farmer during his off time from work. While coming home one night, my father got attacked in the dark by three men who were his so-called friends. They murdered him and put him next to the train tracks to pretend like the train killed him. Everyone in our circle knew that the train did not kill him, because his body would have been severely damaged.

It was summer, and we were off from school. One of my nieces and I were supposed to go to Kingston for summer vacation. I woke up that morning, and Mom told me our Dad did not come home. A bearer came to call him to investigate the murder of a man found dead near the train track crossing, and minutes later, another one came to report it was my father. It was like my world came caving under! I was numb and shocked at the same time. I loved my father so much because he was a great father and a great husband to my mom. He was hardworking, fun-loving, joyful, and playful, and could give his shirt off his back. My father's death affected me so badly; I was truly hurting, and missed the funeral, including the celebration after the burial.

I was inside the house babysitting one of my nephews while crying, and apparently, no one realized I was missing. I realized everyone was caught up in the moment. I was mourning, and time seemed to pass by so fast. His death affected me so badly because I also did not get to see his body before the burial. I was trying to process the entire thing in my little 12 years old head. I internalized and carried that hurt for many years. I avoided going back to Jamaica to visit, mainly because of these traumas.

In 2017 I decided to visit with my family for the tomb rebuilding gathering for him and other family members that passed. I broke down crying next to his tomb for a while; I just could not hold it back. After breaking down crying, I received closure. I realized I internalized his death because I did not have closure. I left it all there at the grave, and I felt better. Eventually, the hurt went away. I learned that it is very important to have closure or come to terms with the traumatic situations in your life in order to heal.

Approximately a year later, we found out from a relative of my father, who lived in a neighboring district, that one of the three men suspected for his murder, was at a bar in that district drinking alcohol and confessed that he and two other men, whose names he mentioned, are responsible for killing my father. The disappointment about these three men is that they were so-called friends of my father, who lived in the neighborhood for years.

Apparently, he could not live with his conscience, and the liquor overcame him. They did not get arrested, because no one reported them or the law was unjust, but karma hit them, and they later died, one after the other. I'm unsure how they passed, because by then, we no longer lived in the district, but family and friends told us when they passed away. My mom was already living in the U.S., and my four younger siblings and I lived with relatives in different towns. My older siblings were already living on their own.

My father's death, my mother's migration to the United States, and me separating from my siblings were a lot for a 12 years old girl to cope with, but I endured. I had to switch my focus to my new life, in a new city, with a new family and school. There was no other choice, I had to grow up. Along the way, I also met some good friends with whom I shared fun times. I realized they too had their stories, but as kids we never talked about the deep and disturbing stuff.

Attempted Rape

Finding a job after high school was difficult in the 80s. I was in pursuit of finding a summer job and, in the process, almost became a rape victim for the second time.

I said almost because I decided it wasn't going down without a fight this time. My friend and I went to a company in Kingston in search of work, but the Security guard guarding the gate told us to return another day. He even told us what day to come back, because according to him, the Manager was not in on this day, but would be there on the date he gave us to come back.

My friend and I planned to return and were supposed

to meet at the gate of the building where we were pursuing jobs. My friend did not show up, so the security guard saw it as an opportunity to take advantage of me in a conniving, sneaky way. I was very naive; therefore, he saw it as an advantage. He told me to follow him to a particular building to meet with the manager. As he took a key out and unlocked the building door, I knew I had been tricked. The door opened into a bedroom. He quickly grabbed me, pushed me onto the bed, and proceeded with attempted rape.

He was harassing me in a very rough way, trying to pull my underwear down, but I would not allow it to happen. I fought with all my strength while letting my voice be heard loudly. I shouted, "get off me!" I kicked and punched him with all my might, because I decided he would not have his way with me, not another rape! It will not happen, not again, not this time. My thoughts about him possibly having a gun didn't even occurred to me, because I was too busy focusing on escaping this rape monster.

During my fighting and yelling, my voice was heard by a man close by who knew him because he called him by his first name. The man came up the stairs and banged on the door several times while calling this monster's name. The monster opened the door to talk to the man knocking the door, who asked him if everything was okay. I didn't wait to listen to his response, and I saw that moment as my big opportunity to escape this monster. I quickly grabbed my handbag, ran past them, and kept running.

I stopped running when I got tired and began walking fast. I glanced behind me and realized this man was walking fast behind me, although he was not too close behind, I could see him; I started running again because I did not trust him, or trust what he would do if he caught up with me. I ran until I was out of sight. I got to my bus stop and took the bus home.

I was so frightened, and was in a state of shock and disbelief. I did not tell anyone about my attempted rape experience. On the bus ride home, I was extremely thankful to God the rape did not occur but was very disappointed in myself for being so naïve and trusting. I couldn't believe I almost got raped again. I did not know what my aunt, cousin or other family members and friends would say, so I decided not to mention the incident to anyone and kept it to myself.

God is definitely stronger than the devil! I knew I was saved by the grace of God, who highly favored me, by sending an angel to my rescue. The man who knocked on the door that day was an angel sent by God. Angels come in all shapes and forms; they do not always come with wings; they walk among us like humans. This man was my human-form angel, sent by my Heavenly Father that day to save me from getting raped in broad daylight. God wants us to, *"Be strong and courageous. Do not fear or be in dread of them, for it is the Lord your God who goes with you. He will not leave you or forsake you." (Deuteronomy 31:6)*

If the enemy had his way, I could have fallen into another trap, but God opened my eyes to see the trap coming. I was waiting at the bus stop for a bus to my destination; these were mini-vans; I was waiting for a mini-van, because they ran more frequently, and they get you to your destination much faster. The man working as the conductor loading people in this van tried to get my attention, while I was standing outside waiting. He began telling me his grandma needed someone to take care of her and that I should come to her home in the van with him.

Right away, I saw a red flag, along with the word trick all over his face. I did not respond to him, but instead quickly walked away to another bus stop to take the public transportation. The minivans were private transportations. The phrase "trouble comes in threes," was not about to be my downfall, oh no, it won't! I could see the perverted look on this man's face, and at this point, after one rape, and an attempted rape, I did not know who to trust.

After getting raped once, the spirit of rape began to

follow me, because whatever demons possessed the two gangsters to rape me, was folllowing me around, attempting to use the bodies of other men to carry out it's evil deeds. Demons can possess your body without you having any knowledge of it. They can make you do things outside your character, you would not normally do. Sometimes you feel down, stressed and depressed, you have anxiety, and basically feel like you are losing, or about to lose your mind; you are in a good mood this minute and the next, you are so very moody and agitated, it might not be your God-given spirit.

Demons are more powerful and forceful when they use people's bodies to do their evil deeds, and the people they are using probably have no clue what is going on with them because it seems like their norm; they believe it's their own spirits. That spirit of rape followed me to the USA and almost got me again on two separate occasions when I went on lunch dates with two guys separately. The first one worked in the mailroom at a company I was working at. We became casual friends, and he asked me to hang out with him for lunch during one of our lunch periods. We sat in my car to eat lunch since it was a short lunchtime. His mood shifted, and I now realized it's quite difficult for some males to be around females alone, especially when there is a physical attraction. The next thing I knew, he tried to hold me down, forcing me to have sex with him. I rejected him, screamed at him, and pushed him away from me. I screamed at him to leave my car, and that was the end of me ever speaking to him again. The thought of reporting him to the company never occurred to me, but he was non-existence to me after that occurrence.

    The next occurrence was similar; it took place in my car as well. This guy was from the same country as me. We knew each other for a while but were never intimate or went out and dated before this occurrence. I met him in the town where I lived because he worked there and used to come into my brother's store to buy breakfast and lunch. I realized he liked me, and I liked him as well. He asked me out on a date in his town. I drove there, we went to see a movie, then to eat. He paid for one; he asked me to pay for the other. I did willingly, but it kinda-a-turned me off since he asked me on the date. I don't mind paying on dates, but if you have no money to pay, do not ask someone on a date unless you both make that mutual arrangement prior to the date; especially the first date. Since I was the one driving, I dropped him off at the parking lot where he lived to be on my way home, but he wanted more and aggressively tried to hold me down in my car, because I rejected him. I pushed him away and yelled at him, he persisted, but I got real serious with him, and he left me alone. I truly thought he was different, since I had known him for a while. I never spoke to him after that, even though he tried reaching out to me. I was so annoyed and disappointed in him, because I thought he knew better; I actually thought he was different. This made me realize how weak some men can be when it comes to their female counterparts, and that I needed to stop trusting them so much.. They took my kindness for weakness, as well as under-estimated me. I was never and still not someone who ran around allowing men to abuse my body. So I had to change my mindset of the kind of men I allowed in my circle. After I re-evaluated myself and changed my mindset, the spirit of rape left me, because God delivered me. He got me covered under His blood, because *"No weapon form against me shall prosper, and every tongue that rises against me in judgment shall be condemned...."(Isaiah 54:17)*.

  Rape is not a Godly thing to do, because the spirit of God will not encourage any human to abuse and take advantage of another human in such a traumatic and abusive way. Raping another human is the mindset of the devil. He will possess another human's mind (soul) to rape a baby, an elderly person, and any human in between. *The enemy comes to kill, steal and destroy, but Jesus comes to give us life, and that we may have life more abundantly (John 10:10)*. God is stronger than the devil, and will definitely not give us more than we can bear.

Molestations

Between ages eleven(11) and eighteen(18), I have been molested by a few male family members and a neighbor, who was married with a wife and children. These incidents took place in Jamaica, before I migrated to the USA. These are grown men who should have known better, and should have protected me. They knew I was vulnerable, and would no doubt be labeled a liar if I vocalized it.

In Jamaica, and around the world, most women do not discuss this issue, because it is shameful and embarrassing, and seems like it's your fault, so you basically keep quiet about it, and move on with your life. This is what happened in my case, I might have spoken about it to a few family members, but it was never discussed. Issues like this usually get swept under the rug. When life throws lemons at you, you basically have to make a bucket of lemonade, roll with the punches, and wait for God to Vindicate you.

Situations like these can either make you or break you. I came to realize in order to be healed, and help others experiencing similar situations, you have to be willing and brave enough to share your story. Although victims are ashamed or forced to be quiet about rape and molestation, it is better to give testimonies or discuss it with others, because you do not know the trauma they are experiencing, and sharing your stories could possibly save their lives. Suppressing the situation can cause depression, anxiety, and other mental health issues. It can cause you to shut down, become quiet and shy, and lose trust for others, especially men. You can feel ashamed, dirty, unwanted, and caused failure to interact or socialize with others. Trauma is not a fun thing to deal with; if you are not mentally strong, it could drive you mentally insane.

My therapy began while watching The Oprah Winfrey Show. I Migrated to the United States in 1983. I loved watching the Oprah Winfrey Show, and could not miss watching an episode when I was not at work. I remembered there was an episode in the early '80s, where Oprah talked about her rape incident, which took place at an early age by an older cousin. She was only nine (9) years old when it started.

Her story truly caught my attention, and I was glued to the TV. I wanted to hear Oprah's story. I then realized I was not alone; that even Oprah, a lady of high status, has experienced rape. It was heart wrenching to me that she was only nine when it occurred; I was sixteen. I couldn't even Phantom that; then I realized kids are being raped at even younger years, as people began telling their stories.

The process of healing began taking place for me,

as Oprah boldly shared her story and experience, I felt as though I could breathe again. At that moment, I no longer felt ashamed. I began to feel like a normal human again. I knew then there was no reason to feel like I have done something wrong, because it was not my fault. My self-esteem began to rise, and I started feeling less oppressed.

I realized then, that I could breathe again, and that it is better to speak about the situation than to cover it up, or suppress it, because millions of men and women experienced rape. Talking about your experience can bring healing not only to you, but to millions of victims who have experienced the same. I was able to come to term with the trauma I experienced, and learned to forgive my abusers. I realized holding a grudge against them forever was only hurting me. Letting go was not the easiest thing to do, but it was the right thing to do, in order to heal.

Coming from Jamaica, a third world country, I never knew women could actually talk about rape as boldly as they do on TV. Oprah has a big platform, which she uses to help many people who have experienced similar situations like her, because she knows it is something women as well as men, do not boldly talk about. It is something that easily gets swept under the rug, because women and men are afraid, ashamed, and do not want to be accused of lying. She exposed her trauma in order to encourage others to expose theirs, in order to experience healing. In most situation, family members are aware their loved ones have experienced rape, but they chose to sweep it under the rug, because they do not want to bring shame to the family. Oftentimes, these rape situations happened within the family, by family members; the ones that should be protecting you.

Romans, 8:28 King James Version stated, "And we know that all things work together for good to them that love God, to them who are called according to his purpose." God has a way for blending things into his plan for us; what the enemies meant for bad, He turned into good. In *Genesis 50:20 NIV*, Joseph said to his brothers *"you intended to harm me, but God intended it for good to accomplish what is now being done, the saving of lives."*

Joseph was sold by his brothers to Potiphar in Egypt. They made their father believe Joseph was eaten by an animal, but he later surfaced after serving years in prison for a crime he did not commit, to save his brothers and the entire family from starvation, due to a 7 years famine, because of the status he gained as second in command to Pharaoh. Ms. Winfrey, after years of rape, has become a great woman of stardom; and has touched and saved many lives, including that of myself using the power, grace, and wisdom our father God instilled in her. Although the experience of trauma can be devastating, you can literally use your story to heal and save the lives of many victims globally.

Bloodline Curses/DNA

Bloodline curses are things that affect our lives just like DNA. Just like DNA comes down from our parents, grandparents and fore-parent/ancestors to affect our genes, the good and bad they do also follow our bloodlines. If there are curses and afflictions over our ancestors' lives coming down to our parents, and those curses have not been prayed for or against, rebuked by us, and canceled and removed by God; those curses can follow and affect our bloodlines until they are broken.

Bloodline curses go all the way back to Adam the first creator who was tempted by Eve; who was tempted by the serpent to eat the apple from the Garden of Eden. They committed sins outside the will of God by disobeying His command. Staying away from sins can only be attained by staying within the will of God. We are all sinners saved by grace, meaning Jesus gave His life as an atonement for our sins. According to *Romans 3:23, we have all sin and come short of the Glory of God.*

God sent His only begotten Son Jesus to bear the Cross for us, so that our sins can be wiped away. *"Behold*

old things have passed away, and behold, all things become new" (2 Corinthians 5:17). God does not use our past to judge us, once we repent from our sins and accept His Son Jesus as our Personal Lord and Savior. In *2 Corinthians 5:17 KJV*, it stated. *"Therefore if any man be in Christ, he is a new creature: Old things have passed away; behold, all things become new"* Our Sins are totally wiped away by God, and He allows us to start anew.

The most divine part of my healing came through an online ministry I have been connected with, called Queen Belemzy Ministries School of Power(QBM-SOP). God touched my life immensely, through Apostle Queen Belemzy. God led me to this great ministry during Five Days of Glory; her 41st birthday celebration, September 29th through October 3rd 2021 in Houston, Texas. Prophet Shamar, whose Ministry I used to follow online at the time, shared a link from 5 Days of Glory to his Live Online Stream; I clicked on it, and it led me to this great woman of God that changed my life in positive ways. Prophet Shamar was invited on Apostle Queen Belemzy's platform as a guest pastor to join her in celebration of her birthday.

After that shared link, I have not stopped watching or following the ministry online. I tried to escape, because I did not think I had the time to be committed to the Ministry, because the videos seemed very long. After continuously watching the videos, I realized, they become more therapeutic. There are lots of healing and deliverance embedded in those videos, as well as listening to the Apostle Queen, because she is so highly anointed by God, who uses her in Supernatural ways to deliver, preach, heal and teach people globally. In this Ministry it's important to repent of your sins, and follow the Ten Commandments as stated in the Bible in *Exodus 20:1-17*

I received the gift of speaking in tongues in October of 2021. I was excited and overwhelmed, felt special and blessed and was happy I could communicate with God in a language the demons do not understand. Speaking in tongues is actually praying in different languages not even you understand, unless God gives you the gift to interpret and understand it. It means the angels are interceding for you, in a language that confuses the devil, because he doesn't understand it; therefore he cannot block your prayers to God.

God Changed My Life & Saved me
God literally used Queen Belemzy Ministries to change my life, with ongoing prayers, teachings, preachings, encouragements, deliverances, praise and worship, reading the Bible always, praying and fastings, as well as other assignments. Apostle Queen does not take credit for

anything God uses her to do, and she forever gives God the Glory, Honor and Praise; which I deeply admire about her.

Chapter 3

Faith and Healing

The role of faith in the healing process

Matthew 9:22 - "Jesus turned and saw her. 'Take heart, daughter,' he said, 'your faith has healed you.' And the woman was healed at that moment."

Hebrews 11:6 - "And without faith it is impossible to please God, because anyone who comes to him must believe that he exists and that he rewards those who earnestly seek him."

One of the most profound aspects of my healing was my faith in God. When I gave my life to Christ, I was still burdened by my past and all the trauma I endured. I recognized that my trauma could be placed at the foot of the cross and my burdens lifted to God. He healed me. The healing was gradual, but eventually; my heart was healed from the pain of my past. If you are dealing with trauma, God is ready to give you the strength to heal. Finding the strength will help you fight the fear, shame, and pain of trauma. *James 5:15 - "And the prayer offered in faith will make the sick person well; the Lord will raise them up. If they have sinned, they will be forgiven."*

The role of faith in the healing process
Faith can be a powerful source of strength and comfort for those who have experienced trauma. It can provide a sense of hope, purpose, and meaning that can help us navigate even the most challenging of circumstances. In this chapter, we will explore the role of faith in the healing process, and offer strategies for deepening our spiritual connection as we journey towards healing and wholeness.

The first step in connecting with our faith is to acknowledge our pain and our need for healing. This means being honest with ourselves and with God about what we have experienced, and recognizing that we cannot heal on our own. We must be willing to open ourselves up to the healing power of God, and to trust that He will guide us on our journey towards wholeness.

The power of prayer and meditation
One way to deepen our spiritual connection is through prayer. Prayer can be a powerful tool for calming the mind and the spirit, and for inviting God into our lives. It can be helpful to set aside time each day for prayer and to create a sacred space where we can connect with God in a meaningful way. This might involve playing worship

music, or simply sitting in silence and allowing ourselves to be still and present. Prayers can heal your heart and strengthen your spirit. Prayers can help you break generational curses and trauma, fight demonic forces, and conquer the vials of the enemy.

Mark 11:24 - "Therefore I tell you, whatever you ask for in prayer, believe that you have received it, and it will be yours."

Meditating on God's word will help your heart heal as you see several women in the bible who had to endure shame, rape, and abuse and how they overcame them. It would also illuminate God's divine promise and covenant to protect us from evil and the devices of the enemy.

Finding strength in scripture

Another way to deepen our spiritual connection is through scripture. The Bible is full of stories of hope, healing, and redemption, and can offer comfort and inspiration during times of struggle. It can be helpful to find passages that speak to our particular struggles, and to reflect on them regularly. This might involve reading a chapter of the Bible each day, or choosing a verse to meditate on throughout the day.

In addition to prayer and scripture, community

can be a powerful source of support and healing. Joining a faith community, such as a church, an online ministry, fellowship, prayer group, or bible study group can provide us with a sense of belonging and connection, as well as opportunities for fellowship and service. It can also provide us with the opportunity to share our struggles and receive support and encouragement from others.

It is important to remember that healing is a process that takes time and patience. It is a journey that requires us to be gentle with ourselves and to trust in God's timing and plan. As we deepen our spiritual connection, we can trust that God will guide us towards the resources and support we need to heal and to thrive. *Psalm 147:3 - "He heals the brokenhearted and binds up their wounds."*

A part of my healing process happened through the School of Power Ministries with Apostle Queen Belema. Her videos brought tremendous changes to my life. Her prayers, encouragement, the way she reads and explains the Bible, and the praise and worship songs are very life changing. It allows me to connect on a personal level with the Holy Spirit. I learned how to fast the correct way for health and spiritual cleansing. For example, when you fast, you need a prayer point; you need to read the Bible and pray, sing songs and worship in order to keep a spiritual connection with Yahweh, so the prayer for your fasting can be answered. Fasting comes with prayer and focusing on the word of God.

I can now fast two to three days straight without food, and sometimes no water. I have done one week fast, ten days fast, fourteen days fast, twenty-one days fast and thirty days fast for spiritual cleansing. I have learned how to have strong faith in God and trust him to fight for me, to go to him always in prayer and fasting, and he will come through for me if it is within his will. I give God all the glory, praise and adoration for always hearing my prayers, and for always coming through for me. I humbly give You the Glory Yahweh.

I was basically dieting without realizing it, because As we navigate life, we'll meet people who impact our lives negatively and positively, but each experience is a learning experience that can become a great message.

God used this supernatural ministry under the direction of the Apostle Queen Belema (AKA Queen Belemzy) called Queen Belemzy Ministries School of Power (QBM-SOP), to be a great instrument of healing for me. I'm able to cope with the experience of rape that caused trauma in my life, and forgive my abusers. When the power of the Holy Spirit dwells in your heart; it makes it easier for you to forgive and love. Love conquers all.

God: The Center of it all.

Through God, all things are possible. He is the center of it all. He's my Creator, Protector, Provider, and Great Mighty healer. He sends Angels to protect me while driving, eating, sleeping and walking.

Isaiah 53:5 - "But he was pierced for our transgressions, he was crushed for our iniquities; the punishment that brought us peace was on him, and by his wounds we are healed."

He gave me Bible scriptures when I was down and crying, or said some calming words, and He continues to do the same. As long as we seek Him, He'll come through for us. We have to let God be God and allow God to do what He does best. God is forever in total control of everything including the crisis we are facing no matter how gruesome and never-ending it seems at the time; we just need to submit to Him and trust that He will fight for us. *"The Lord shall fight for you, and ye shall hold your peace." (Exodus. 44:14, KJV).*

God is always there with open arms to receive us. He will not chase after us, we have to go to Him, and submit to Him. Let's face it, God is our creator, He doesn't need us, we need Him, but He wants His children to come to Him, talk to Him, show Him love and respect, and surrender all to Him. Actually, He should be our first love, for without Him, we are nothing.

God will make the impossible or what seems impossible, possible. According to *Mark 9:23 KJV"*, *"If you can believe, all things are possible to him who believes."* God is our mighty healer and deliverer, and can make the wrong things right, if we let him. God is a rewarder of those who do good.

Faith After Trauma

Life is unpredictable, and it can be challenging to navigate at times. We all face different forms of obstacles, trauma, and pain, and it's easy to feel defeated and overwhelmed. However, it's essential to remember that you are not alone, and there is always hope. With the right mindset, support, and faith, you can overcome anything and live a fulfilling life.

Trauma can come in many forms, and it can be difficult to deal with the aftermath. Rape and abuse are two of the most traumatic experiences anyone can go through, and they can leave lasting emotional and physical scars. However, it's important to know that healing is possible. The journey to healing may be long and challenging, but it's worth it in the end. You are not defined by what has happened to you and are not alone. Seek help from a therapist, support group, faith-based community, or trusted loved ones. The healing process may involve facing difficult emotions and memories, but with time and effort, you can learn to manage them and move forward.

When faced with obstacles, it's easy to feel discouraged and defeated. However, it's crucial to adopt a positive and resilient mindset. Instead of focusing on what you can't do, focus on what you can do. Set small goals for yourself and celebrate each achievement. Take time to reflect on your strengths and abilities, and use them to your advantage. Remember that setbacks are part of the journey, and they don't define your worth or potential. Keep moving forward, and don't give up on yourself.

Faith is a powerful tool that can provide comfort and strength in difficult times. Believing in a higher power can help you find meaning and purpose, and provide a sense of hope and peace. It's important to nurture your relationship with God and seek guidance and support through prayer and meditation. Surround yourself with like-minded individuals who share your beliefs and can provide encouragement and accountability. Remember that God loves you unconditionally and is always with you, even in the darkest moments.

In addition to faith, self-love and self-care are essential components of healing and overcoming obstacles. Take time to care for your physical, emotional, and spiritual needs. Practice healthy habits such as exercise, eating well, and getting enough rest. Set boundaries and say no to things that drain your energy or cause you stress. Spend time doing things that bring you joy and fulfillment. Nurturing yourself will help you feel more confident, resilient, and capable of facing challenges.

Life can be difficult, but it's important to remember that you have the strength and resilience to overcome anything. Seek help, nurture your faith, practice self-care, and adopt a positive and resilient mindset. Remember that healing takes time and effort, but it's possible. Focus on your strengths and abilities, and don't let setbacks define your worth or potential. With the right tools and support, you can overcome obstacles, win after trauma, deal with the pain of rape and abuse, and love God. You are not alone, and there is always hope.

If you have gotten this far, praise God. In the next few chapters, we will explore practical tools for managing symptoms of trauma, and for creating a sense of safety and stability in our lives. Through these tools, we can begin to move towards a greater sense of healing and wholeness.

1 Peter 2:24 - "He himself bore our sins in his body on the cross, so that we might die to sins and live for righteousness; by his wounds you have been healed."

Chapter 4

Overcoming Obstacles

Recognizing and confronting obstacles to healing

Isaiah 43:2 - "When you pass through the waters, I will be with you; and through the rivers, they shall not overwhelm you; when you walk through fire you shall not be burned, and the flame shall not consume you."

Trauma can have a profound impact on our physical, emotional, and psychological well-being. It can cause us to feel disconnected from ourselves and from the world around us, and can lead to symptoms such as anxiety, depression, and insomnia.

One of the most effective tools for managing symptoms of trauma is mindfulness. Mindfulness involves being present and fully engaged in the current moment, without judgment or distraction. It can help us to become more aware of our thoughts and feelings, and to develop a sense of self-compassion and self-awareness. This can be particularly helpful for managing symptoms such as anxiety and depression.

Another important tool for managing symptoms of trauma is exercise. Exercise has been shown to have a powerful impact on our physical and emotional well-being, and can help to reduce symptoms of anxiety and depression. It can also help to regulate our nervous system and to create a sense of grounding and stability in our bodies.

In addition to mindfulness and exercise, it can be helpful to create a sense of safety and stability in our daily lives. This might involve developing a routine that includes regular meal times, exercise, and sleep. It might also involve creating a calming and nurturing environment in our homes, with things such as soft lighting, soothing music, and comfortable furniture. Prayer is essential in overcoming obstacles and dealing with the scars of trauma. *Philippians 4:13 - "I can do all things through Christ who strengthens me."*

God can strengthen you as you go through the pain of trauma more than any of these things can. He has given us authority to overcome all the devices and arrows shot by the devil; we only need to rely and trust in Him. *Psalm 121:1-2 says, "I lift up my eyes to the hills, from whence comes my help. My help comes from the Lord, who made Heaven and earth."*

The Lord does not sleep nor slumber, He is always aware of the pain we are going through and He cares for us. I take comfort in this Song of Ascents written by David in *Psalm 121*:

I lift up my eyes to the hills-- where does my help come from?

My help comes from the LORD, the Maker of heaven and earth.

He will not let your foot slip-- he who watches over you will not slumber;

Indeed, he who watches over Israel will neither slumber nor sleep.

The LORD watches over you-- the LORD is your shade at your right hand;

the sun will not harm you by day, nor the moon by night.

The LORD will keep you from all harm-- he will watch over your life;

the LORD will watch over your coming and going both now and forevermore.

We are more than conquerors through Christ and through His divine intervention we WIN. God also has provided so much healing support through the help of spiritual advisors, mentors, support groups, counselors, therapists, etc. It can be helpful to seek out support from others who have experienced trauma. The Bible says iron sharpens iron, and connecting with others who have dealt with trauma can be the healing you need. By sharing our experiences with others, we can feel less alone and more understood and can gain valuable insights and perspectives on our healing journey.

While managing symptoms of trauma can be challenging, it is important to remember that healing is possible. With the right tools and support, we can begin to create a sense of safety and stability in our lives, and to move towards greater feelings of peace and wholeness.

I did many things to occupy my time and to keep my mind focused. I got up early in the mornings to exercise before going to work. For me, running is one of my favorite means of exercise. I ran on the treadmill for approximately 15 mins, rode the exercise bike for 5 minutes, did stretches for 5 minutes, did sit-ups for 5 minutes, and sometimes I would go walking with my friends after work. I made sure to treat myself to manicures and pedicures at least twice per month, and treated myself at the mall. I am a big shoe lover, so I was always looking at shoes or sneakers to buy.

I listened to gospel music while driving and sang along with it. I read motivational books to uplift my spirit, as well as spiritual books of people who experienced trauma and overcame it. One favorite book I read was, "Embraced by the Light," It spoke of a woman who had a near death experience, and came back to tell a very inspirational story. She mentioned, there is no stronger prayer to God than that of a mother about her children.

As I reconnect with my family in The U.S. after separation in Jamaica, my mind became more occupied. Since I am from a big family, there were always some sort of celebrations going on, like birthday parties, graduation ceremonies, graduation parties, and summer cookouts at the park, or in our backyards. Church became a regular Sunday routine for me, so I would attend with family members, as well as attend or take part in programs.

Sometimes I would work two jobs, or work one job while going to school, because that was therapy for me. The healing process was not overnight for me, but I relied on God's Grace and kept the faith, He will come through for me. Sometimes when I thought about it I cried, because I am only human, but I did not sit around feeling sorry for myself and made excuses, not to do things. You can allow trauma to either make you, or break you, but I decided to choose the latter. I knew in my heart that God is always with me, and I hold on to that belief.

Romans 8:28 says, "And we know that in all things God works for the good of those who love him, who have been called according to his purpose."

ALL THINGS work together for my good and

your good. Not just SOME THINGS but ALL THINGS, meaning all my trauma, the rape, the grief of loss, the pain, the failure, ALL OF THESE THINGS work together for my good because I am called according to His purpose. So rather than feeling sorry for myself, I focus on the greatest healer, Jesus.

James 1:2-4 - "Consider it pure joy, my brothers and sisters, whenever you face trials of many kinds, because you know that the testing of your faith produces perseverance. Let perseverance finish its work so that you may be mature and complete, not lacking anything."

God's grace is always sufficient for everyone who is dealing with the pain of trauma, according to *2 Corinthians 12:9-10 - "But he said to me, 'My grace is sufficient for you, for my power is made perfect in weakness.' Therefore I will boast all the more gladly about my weaknesses, so that Christ's power may rest on me. That is why, for Christ's sake, I delight in weaknesses, in insults, in hardships, in persecutions, in difficulties. For when I am weak, then I am strong."*

Have faith in God's ability to heal you and deliver you. *Hebrews 11:1 - "Now faith is confidence in what we hope for and assurance about what we do not see."*

These scriptures remind us that God is with us, and that we can do all things through Christ who strengthens us. They encourage us to trust in God's plan for our lives and to persevere through trials, knowing that our faith produces perseverance and that we will ultimately be made complete and lacking nothing.

Chapter 5

Forgiveness and Compassion

Cultivating Healing and Wholeness

Colossians 3:13 - "Bear with each other and forgive one another if any of you has a grievance against someone. Forgive as the Lord forgave you."
1 Peter 3:8-9 - "Finally, all of you, be like-minded, be sympathetic, love one another, be compassionate and humble. Do not repay evil with evil or insult with insult. On the contrary, repay evil with blessing, because to this you were called so that you may inherit a blessing."

Forgiveness can be extremely difficult, if you are honest with yourself. God forgives, Jesus doesn't hold a grudge because even after He was hung on a cross, He forgave the people who crucified Him. That is amazing. It took me a long time to heal from my trauma and longer to forgive those who committed the crime. But Jesus asked us to forgive as the Lord forgave. We are to release our hurt into God's hands and let Him soften our heart toward forgiveness.

Matthew 6:14-15 says, "For if you forgive other people when they sin against you, your heavenly Father will also forgive you. But if you do not forgive others their sins, your Father will not forgive your sins."

Trauma can cause us to feel a range of difficult emotions, including anger, resentment, and bitterness. These emotions can be particularly directed towards those who have hurt us, and can create a sense of distance and disconnection in our relationships.

Joseph was the favorite son of Jacob, which made his brothers jealous. In their envy, they plotted to kill him, but eventually sold him into slavery in Egypt instead. Joseph was then falsely accused of a crime and thrown into prison for years, but eventually rose to a position of power in Pharaoh's court, where he was able to use his position to help his family during a famine.

When Joseph's brothers came to Egypt seeking food, they didn't recognize him, but he recognized them. Joseph could have taken revenge on his brothers for what they had done to him, but instead, he showed them compassion and forgiveness. He revealed his identity to them and said, *"Do not be distressed and do not be angry with yourselves for selling me here, because it was to save lives, and God sent me ahead of you." (Genesis 45:5)*

Joseph forgave his brothers for the harm they had caused him and used his position to provide for them and their families. He even invited them to come and live with him in Egypt, where he promised to care for them.

The lesson we can learn from Joseph's story is that forgiveness is a powerful tool for healing after trauma. Joseph could have harbored anger and resentment towards his brothers, but instead, he chose to extend compassion and forgiveness towards them. In doing so, he was able to heal the wounds of the past and bring reconciliation to his family.

Similarly, when we experience trauma, it can be easy to hold onto bitterness and anger towards those who have hurt us. But holding onto these feelings only perpetuates the trauma and keeps us from experiencing healing and wholeness. By choosing to forgive, we can break free from the cycle of trauma and open ourselves up to the healing power of God's love and grace.

Forgiveness is a process of letting go of anger, resentment, and bitterness towards those who have hurt us. It does not mean forgetting what has happened or excusing the behavior of the person who hurt us. Rather, it means choosing to release our negative emotions and focusing on moving forward positively and healthily. God wants us to forgive. Even our savior, the Lord Jesus Christ forgave those who crucified Him on the cross. He urges us to forgive others no matter how horrible they treated us. Forgiveness frees us of the burden of holding on the pain caused by someone else.

Letting go of the pain helps us move past the trauma it caused. I chose to forgive my abusers, because I understood they were lost and needed a savior. It was not them in the actual sense that committed the heinous crime but the devil in them. *"For we wrestle not against flesh and blood, but against principalities, against powers, against the rulers of the darkness of this world, against spiritual wickedness in high places." Ephesians 6:12*

One of the first steps in cultivating forgiveness is to acknowledge our pain and to give ourselves permission to feel the difficult emotions that come with it. This means being honest with ourselves and with God about our struggles and recognizing that our emotions are a natural and normal response to what we have experienced.

Another important step in cultivating forgiveness is to practice self-compassion. Self-compassion involves treating ourselves with the same kindness, care, and understanding that we would offer to a good friend. It means acknowledging our mistakes and imperfections and offering ourselves the love and support that we need to heal and grow. Whoever would foster love covers over an offense, but whoever repeats the matter separates close friends. *Proverbs 17:9*

Psalm 103:8 - "The Lord is compassionate and gracious, slow to anger, abounding in love."

In addition to self-compassion, it can be helpful to practice compassion towards others. Compassion involves recognizing that everyone, including those who have hurt us, is struggling in their own way. It means choosing to see the humanity and worth in others and to extend love and forgiveness even when it is difficult.

Sin lives in humans and the devil uses humans to fulfill evil on earth if they do not give themselves over to the saving grace of God. *Romans 7:16-18* tells us that *sin dwells in us, v.16. And if I do what I do not want to do, I admit that the law is good. v.17. In that case, it is no longer I who does it, but it is sin living in me that does it. v. 18. I know that nothing good lives in me, that is, in my flesh; for I have the desire to do what is good, but I cannot carry it out.*

Forgiving those who hurt us might be difficult but that's what God is asking of us. *Ephesians 4:31-32 - "Get rid of all bitterness, rage and anger, brawling and slander, along with every form of malice. Be kind and compassionate to one another, forgiving each other, just as Christ God forgave you."*

It is important to remember that forgiveness is a journey, not a destination. It takes time and effort to cultivate forgiveness and compassion, and it may require seeking support from others, such as a therapist or spiritual advisor. However, by choosing to release our negative emotions and to focus on healing and growth, we can begin to experience greater feelings of peace, joy, and wholeness in our lives. *Luke 6:37 - "Do not judge, and you will not be judged. Do not condemn, and you will not be condemned. Forgive, and you will be forgiven."*

One thing that also helped me was the power of gratitude and positivity in the healing process; God gave me strategies for cultivating gratitude and finding joy and meaning in life. Through these practices, I began to shift my focus towards the positive and to experience greater feelings of well-being and happiness. *Rejoice always, pray without ceasing, in everything give thanks; for this is the will of God in Christ Jesus for you. 1 Thessalonians 5:16-18 (NKJV)*

Chapter 6

Loving God through the Pain

Psalm 34:18 - "The Lord is close to the brokenhearted and saves those who are crushed in spirit."

Trauma can shake our faith and cause us to question God's love and care for us. In this chapter, we will explore the ways in which we can continue to love God through the pain and deepen our relationship with Him even in the midst of difficult circumstances. *Isaiah 43:2 says, "When you pass through the waters, I will be with you; and through the rivers, they shall not overwhelm you; when you walk through fire you shall not be burned, and the flame shall not consume you."*

One of the first steps in loving God through the pain is to acknowledge and express our emotions honestly and openly. This means being honest with God about our struggles, and allowing ourselves to feel a range of emotions, including anger, confusion, and doubt. *Hebrews 12:1-2 - "Therefore, since we are surrounded by such a great cloud of witnesses, let us throw off everything that hinders and the sin that so easily entangles. And let us run with perseverance the race marked out for us, fixing our eyes on Jesus, the pioneer and perfecter of faith. For the joy set before Him He endured the cross, scorning its shame, and sat down at the right hand of the throne of God."*

It also means recognizing that our emotions are not a reflection of our faith but rather a natural response to the difficult circumstances we are facing. It is okay to feel those emotions but we have to be ready to let them go. *Romans 8:28 - "And we know that in all things God works for the good of those who love him, who have been called according to his purpose."*

Another important step in loving God through the pain is to seek out support and encouragement from others in our faith community. We can simply spend time with others who share our beliefs and values. By connecting with others who can offer us support, guidance, and encouragement, we can strengthen our faith and find greater hope and meaning in our struggles. *Psalm 23:4 - "Even though I walk through the darkest valley, I will fear no evil, for you are with me; your rod and your staff, they comfort me."*

2 Corinthians 12:9-10 - "But he said to me, 'My

grace is sufficient for you, for my power is made perfect in weakness.' Therefore I will boast all the more gladly about my weaknesses, so that Christ's power may rest on me. That is why, for Christ's sake, I delight in weaknesses, in insults, in hardships, in persecutions, in difficulties. For when I am weak, then I am strong."

James 1:12 - "Blessed is the one who perseveres under trial because, having stood the test, that person will receive the crown of life that the Lord has promised to those who love him."

In addition to seeking out support from others, it can be helpful to spend time in prayer and reflection, and to cultivate a sense of gratitude and awe towards God. This might involve spending time in nature, meditating on scripture, or simply taking time to reflect on the blessings and gifts that God has given us. By focusing on the positive aspects of our faith and recognizing the ways in which God is present in our lives, we can deepen our love and connection to Him.

Finally, it is important to remember that loving God through the pain is a journey, and one that may involve ups and downs, setbacks and triumphs. However, by continuing to seek out His presence and guidance, and by cultivating a sense of gratitude and connection to our faith community, we can find greater strength, peace, and meaning in our lives, even in the midst of difficult circumstances.

In the final chapter, we will explore the ways in which we can continue to grow and heal in our journey towards wholeness and peace. Through the practices and tools we have explored in this book, we can begin to create a sense of safety, healing, and growth in our lives, and move towards greater feelings of peace, joy, and wholeness.

Chapter 7

Sharing Your Story

The Message in your Mess

Psalm 107:2 - "Let the redeemed of the Lord tell their story—those he redeemed from the hand of the foe."
2 Corinthians 1:3-4 - "Praise be to the God and Father of our Lord Jesus Christ, the Father of compassion and the God of all comfort, who comforts us in all our troubles, so that we can comfort those in any trouble with the comfort we ourselves receive from God."

God often uses our mess to glorify His name. He uses our stories to inspire others and help others heal and not feel alone. Trauma can be isolating and can leave us feeling alone and disconnected from others. Sharing our story can be a powerful way to break the cycle of isolation and shame that often accompanies trauma. By speaking openly and honestly about our experiences, we can begin to connect with others who have gone through similar struggles and find a sense of support, validation, and understanding.

Revelation 12:11 says, - "They triumphed over him by the blood of the Lamb and by the word of their testimony; they did not love their lives so much as to shrink from death." Our testimonies and sharing our message of healing and victory frees and heals us. We overcome the pain of trauma through the words of our testimony. Oftentimes, we want to hide our mess and want to look perfect to the world. But God wants us to share our story so we can help others heal. *Mark 5:19 - "Go home to your own people and tell them how much the Lord has done for you, and how he has had mercy on you."*

However, sharing our story can also be a difficult and vulnerable process, and it is important to approach it with care and intention. Ask God for help to lead you and to give you wisdom on how and when to share your story. Pray for Him to strengthen your heart during this process. Don't just share your story for sharing sake; ask God to use your story to heal others, help others speak up, and deter predators from victimizing others. The Bible is filled with individuals God used despite their mess. He is not calling perfect humans to shine their light but imperfect humans to shine their light through the darkness. *Psalm 66:16 - "Come and hear, all you who fear God; let me tell you what he has done for me."*

One of the first steps in sharing our story is to find

a safe and supportive environment in which to do so. This might involve talking with a trusted friend or family member, joining a support group, or working with a therapist who specializes in trauma.

In addition to finding a safe and supportive environment, it is important to approach the sharing of your story with self-compassion and care. This means recognizing your own limits and boundaries and being honest with yourself about what you are comfortable sharing and when. It also means recognizing that we are not responsible for the reactions of others and that it is okay to set boundaries and take care of ourselves if we feel overwhelmed or triggered.

Another important aspect of sharing your story is to approach it with a sense of purpose and intention. This might involve identifying the reasons why you want to share your story, and what you hope to gain from doing so. It might also involve thinking about the impact that sharing your story might have on others, and how you can use your experiences to help and support others who are going through similar struggles.

It is important to remember that sharing your story is a process, and one that may involve both ups and downs. However, by approaching it with care, intention, and self-compassion, you can begin to break the cycle of isolation and shame that often accompanies trauma, and find greater feelings of connection, support, and healing in your lives. God wanted me to make my petition known because many women as well as men have and are still experiencing similar situations.

Telling my story might help them to make their petition known as well in order to bring closure to this horrific pain and trauma, and be healed mentally, physically, spiritual, and emotionally. Exposing this horrible demon can help us let go of the bitterness, and bring a sense of calm and peace to the spirits (heart) and soul (mind). May you garner the strength to share your story at the right time and maybe through your story someone else can be healed and saved.

Chapter 8

Moving Forward

Finding hope and joy in the future

Philippians 3:13-14 - "Brothers and sisters, I do not consider myself yet to have taken hold of it. But one thing I do: Forgetting what is behind and straining toward what is ahead, I press on toward the goal to win the prize for which God has called me Heavenward in Christ Jesus."

Dealing with trauma can be a challenging and overwhelming experience, but it's essential to move forward from it. As a woman of God, I believe nothing can be done outside of God's divine intervention. I moved forward after all the trauma I had to deal with and the pain I suffered. But there are practical ways to move forward, some I will share below. The most important one is PRAYER. Pray to God to help you move past the pain the trauma has caused. Ask God to deliver you from any spiritual deposits. Seek deliverance if you can to rid yourself of all or any demonic deposits in your body, spirit, or soul. *Matthew 17:21 (NKJV) However, this kind does not go out except by prayer and fasting."*

These practical ways can help as you move past your pain and start life anew.

Acknowledge the Trauma: The first step in moving forward is to acknowledge the trauma you've experienced. You can't heal what you don't acknowledge, so take some time to reflect on what happened and how it's affected you.

Seek Professional Help: Trauma can leave deep emotional wounds that require professional help to heal. Don't be afraid to seek the support of a therapist, counselor, or mental health professional. They can provide you with the tools and resources you need to heal and move forward.

Practice Self-Care: Self-care is essential when dealing with trauma. Take care of yourself physically, emotionally, and spiritually. This includes eating healthy, getting enough sleep, exercising, and practicing self-compassion.

Surround Yourself With Positive Influences: Surround yourself with people who support and encourage you. Avoid negative influences that can trigger trauma and bring you down.

Set Goals: Setting goals for the future can help you move forward and provide a sense of purpose. Start with small goals and work your way up. Celebrate each accomplishment along the way.

Forgive Yourself and Others: Forgiveness is a powerful tool that can help you move forward. Forgiveness doesn't mean forgetting, but it means letting go of the anger and resentment that holds you back. Forgive yourself and others for the pain caused by trauma and free yourself from the weight of the past.

Trust in God: Trust in God's plan for your life and know that he has a purpose for you. Lean on him for comfort and strength as you move forward. Remember that he is always with you, even in the darkest moments.

Isaiah 43:18-19 - "Forget the former things; do not dwell on the past. See, I am doing a new thing! Now it springs up; do you not perceive it? I am making a way in the wilderness and streams in the wasteland." Moving forward from trauma is a process that takes time and effort, but it's possible. With the right mindset, support, and resources, you can heal from trauma and start a new chapter in life. Remember that you're not alone and that God is with you every step of the way. *Proverbs 4:25-26 - "Let your eyes look straight ahead; fix your gaze directly before you. Give careful thought to the paths for your feet and be steadfast in all your ways."*

Don't let the pain of your past destroy your future. Let God soothe your aching heart and give you a joy renewed daily. God does not delight in your pain, neither is He interested in seeing your suffering, or having anxiety about your life. *Philippians 4:6-7 - "Do not be anxious about anything, but in every situation, by prayer and petition, with thanksgiving, present your requests to God. And the peace of God, which transcends all understanding, will guard your hearts and your minds in Christ Jesus."*

Stay focused on Him and fortify yourself with prayer. Let your words go to God so He can heal you. *Psalm 37:23-24 - "The Lord makes firm the steps of the one who delights in him; though he may stumble, he will not fall, for the Lord upholds him with his hand."*

Romans 12:12 - "Be joyful in hope, patient in affliction, faithful in prayer."

Hebrews 12:1-2 - "Therefore, since we are surrounded by such a great cloud of witnesses, let us throw off everything that hinders and the sin that so easily entangles. And let us run with perseverance the race marked out for us, fixing our eyes on Jesus, the pioneer and perfecter of faith."

These scriptures remind us to let go of the past and focus on the present and future, to trust in God's plan for our lives, to be patient and faithful in prayer, and to persevere in the race marked out for us. They also assure us that even when we stumble, God will uphold us and make our paths straight.

Conclusion

In this book, we have explored the challenges and opportunities of overcoming trauma through the power of faith and community. We have seen that healing from trauma is a process that requires intention, care, and patience, but that it is also possible through the support and guidance of those around us.

Throughout the book, we have explored a range of strategies and tools for overcoming trauma, including building a support network, cultivating self-compassion and resilience, engaging in practices of gratitude and awe, and sharing our story with others. While these strategies may look different for each person, they are all rooted in the power of faith and community to heal and transform our lives.

In reflecting on our journey, it is important to remember that healing from trauma is not a one-time event, but rather a journey that requires ongoing attention and care. However, through the practices and tools we have explored in this book, we can begin to create a sense of safety, healing, and growth in our lives, and move towards greater feelings of peace, joy, and wholeness.

Above all, we have seen that the key to overcoming trauma is to stay connected to the power of faith and community, and to remember that we are not alone in our struggles. By cultivating a sense of gratitude and awe towards God, and by seeking out the support and guidance of others in our faith community, we can find the strength and resilience we need to move towards a life of greater healing, growth, and connection.

Scriptures

Here are some Scriptures that can offer comfort, hope, and healing to those who have experienced trauma:

Psalm 34:18 - "The Lord is close to the brokenhearted and saves those who are crushed in spirit."

Isaiah 41:10 - "So do not fear, for I am with you; do not be dismayed, for I am your God. I will strengthen you and help you; I will uphold you with my righteous right hand."

Psalm 23:4 - "Even though I walk through the darkest valley, I will fear no evil, for you are with me; your rod and your staff, they comfort me."

Matthew 11:28-30 - "Come to me, all you who are weary and burdened, and I will give you rest. Take my yoke upon you and learn from me, for I am gentle and humble in heart, and you will find rest for your souls. For my yoke is easy and my burden is light."

Romans 8:28 - "And we know that in all things God works for the good of those who love him, who have been called according to his purpose."

Isaiah 53:4-5 - "Surely he took up our pain and bore our suffering, yet we considered him punished by God, stricken by him, and afflicted. But he was pierced for our transgressions, he was crushed for our iniquities; the punishment that brought us peace was on him, and by his wounds we are healed."

Philippians 4:6-7 - "Do not be anxious about anything, but in every situation, by prayer and petition, with thanksgiving, present your requests to God. And the peace of God, which transcends all understanding, will guard your hearts and your minds in Christ Jesus."

2 Corinthians 1:3-4 - "Praise be to the God and Father of our Lord Jesus Christ, the Father of compassion and the God of all comfort, who comforts us in all our troubles, so that we can comfort those in any trouble with the comfort we ourselves receive from God."

Psalm 147:3 - "He heals the brokenhearted and binds up their wounds."

Isaiah 61:1 - "The Spirit of the Sovereign Lord is on me, because the Lord has anointed me to proclaim good news to the poor. He has sent me to bind up the brokenhearted, to proclaim freedom for the captives and release from darkness for the prisoners."

These scriptures can offer hope, comfort, and guidance to those who have experienced trauma, reminding them that they are not alone, and that God is always present to heal and restore.

Prayers

Here are some prayers for those dealing with trauma:

Prayer for Comfort:

Heavenly Father, I come to you today to ask for your comfort and peace to surround those dealing with trauma. Lord, you know the pain and hurt that they are feeling, and I pray that you would wrap your loving arms around them and bring them a sense of calm. Please help them to feel your presence and to know that you are with them through this difficult time. In Jesus' name, I pray. Amen.

Prayer for Healing:

Dear God, I pray for those who are dealing with trauma and ask that you would bring them healing. Lord, you are a great physician, and I ask that You touch them with your healing hand and restore them to wholeness. I pray that you would heal the physical, emotional, and spiritual wounds that they are experiencing and that you would bring them a sense of peace and restoration. In Jesus' name, I pray. Amen.

Prayer for Strength:

Heavenly Father, I pray for those who are dealing with trauma and ask that you would give them the strength they need to face each day. Lord, you know the weight that they are carrying, and I pray that you will give them the courage to keep moving forward. Please give them the strength to face their fears and the hope to know that they can overcome this trauma with your help. In Jesus' name, I pray. Amen.

Prayer for Peace:

Dear God, I pray for those who are dealing with trauma and ask that you would bring them a sense of peace. Lord, I know that their hearts and minds are filled with worry and anxiety, and I ask that you would calm their fears and give them a sense of tranquility. Please help them to find rest and peace in you and to know that you are in control. In Jesus' name, I pray. Amen.

Prayer for Guidance:

Heavenly Father, I pray for those who are dealing with trauma and ask that you would guide them in the right direction. Lord, they are facing a difficult and uncertain road, and I ask that you would give them wisdom and discernment as they navigate this journey. Please help them to know the steps to take and the decisions to make, and to trust in your guidance and provision. In Jesus' name, I pray. Amen.

Salvation prayer

Father Lord I come into Your presence as a sinner.

I confess all my sins.

Please forgive me.

I didn't know any better.

I promise not to go back to my old ways.

I believe that Jesus Christ came and died for me, on the cross of calvary, so that my sins can be wiped away.

I accept Jesus Christ as my Lord and Personal Savior.

Be the Lord over my life.

I promise to serve You forever and ever.

In the name of Jesus! Amen!

About the Author

Vinnette Smart-Bruney is a woman of God, and has a personal relationship with God. She was born in Manchester, Jamaica, West Indies. In Jamaica, she attended Harry Watch all Age School in Harry Watch Manchester, Windward Road All Age School in Kingston, and St. Hugh's High School in Kingston. She is one of 15 children, to include 7 boys and 8 girls, born to Imogene and Rudolph Smart. She immigrated to the United States in 1983.

She has a husband Claytus for 33 years, and together they have two sons, Romaine and Kadeem, and a grandson named Cole; son to Romaine. She was deeply involved in the education and sports activities for both sons, who kept her extremely busy, because they wanted to play almost every sport. She decided to go back to college to pursue her education while both sons were in college.

Vinnette obtained an MBA with Global Management concentration, a Bachelor's in Healthcare Administration, with a Minor in Psychology, from Ashford University, while working full time as a Senior Surgery Coordinator, coordinating surgeries for varieties of specialists, focusing mainly on Orthopedics, and she did both while caring for her elderly mother. Vinnette also worked as a Medical Billing and Collections Supervisor. After migrating from Jamaica, She attended a cosmetology school, and obtained her cosmetology license. She also worked as a banker, before branching off into the medical field.

Vinnette enjoyed charity works, because she loves giving and helping others. She will give the last dollar in her wallet to someone in need. She enjoys counseling others, especially children. She has great love for children and loves to see them happy at all times. Vinnette enjoys reading, writing, dancing, listening to music, running, watching track and field and traveling.

How Vinnette Would Like To Be Remembered
Vinnette would like to be remembered as the God-Fearing Woman who travels the World to help Bridge the Gap of Hunger, Homelessness, Clothing and Education, regardless of Race, Religion or Nationality. Someone who spreads Light, Love and Joy to the World. Vinnette believes we are all here on assignments for God, and the sooner we discover what our purpose or assignments are, the better our lives and the World will be.

www.ingramcontent.com/pod-product-compliance
Lightning Source LLC
Chambersburg PA
CBHW041130110526
44592CB00020B/2757